Taste of Italy: 50 Authentic Recipes from the Heart of Italy

By: Kelly Johnson

Table of Contents

- Margherita Pizza
- Spaghetti Carbonara
- Lasagna alla Bolognese
- Risotto alla Milanese
- Caprese Salad
- Fettuccine Alfredo
- Gnocchi with Pesto
- Osso Buco
- Eggplant Parmesan
- Tiramisu
- Bruschetta with Tomatoes and Basil
- Frittata with Spinach and Cheese
- Vitello Tonnato
- Panzanella Salad
- Ravioli with Ricotta and Spinach
- Minestrone Soup
- Focaccia Bread
- Polenta with Mushrooms
- Marinated Artichokes
- Cacciatore Chicken
- Bucatini all'Amatriciana
- Arancini (Stuffed Rice Balls)
- Cannoli
- Ricotta Cheesecake
- Porchetta
- Farro Salad with Vegetables
- Sicilian Caponata
- Pasta Primavera
- Risotto with Seafood
- Pappardelle with Wild Boar Ragù
- Zuppa Toscana
- Semifreddo
- Neapolitan Pizza Margherita
- Baked Ziti
- Cicchetti (Venetian Tapas)

- Stuffed Zucchini Flowers
- Gnocchi alla Sorrentina
- Sicilian Cannoli
- Torta della Nonna
- Carbonara with Pecorino Romano
- Fagioli all'Uccelletto
- Italian Meatballs in Marinara Sauce
- Pasta alla Norma
- Baked Eggplant with Tomato Sauce
- Saffron Risotto with Shrimp
- Pizzelle (Italian Waffle Cookies)
- Saltimbocca alla Romana
- Limoncello Sorbet
- Insalata di Mare (Seafood Salad)
- Cantucci with Vin Santo

Margherita Pizza

Ingredients:

- 1 pizza dough (store-bought or homemade)
- 1/2 cup tomato sauce
- 1 1/2 cups fresh mozzarella cheese, sliced
- Fresh basil leaves
- Olive oil, for drizzling
- Salt and pepper to taste

Instructions:

Preheat the oven to 475°F (245°C). Roll out the pizza dough on a floured surface to your desired thickness. Spread a thin layer of tomato sauce on top. Arrange the mozzarella slices evenly over the sauce. Sprinkle with salt and pepper. Bake for 10-12 minutes, or until the crust is golden and the cheese is melted. After baking, top with fresh basil leaves and drizzle with olive oil before serving.

Spaghetti Carbonara

Ingredients:

- 12 oz spaghetti
- 4 oz pancetta or guanciale, diced
- 2 large eggs
- 1/2 cup grated Parmesan cheese
- 1/2 cup grated Pecorino Romano cheese
- Salt and pepper to taste
- Fresh parsley, for garnish

Instructions:

Cook the spaghetti according to the package instructions. While the pasta cooks, sauté the pancetta in a skillet over medium heat until crispy. In a bowl, whisk together the eggs, Parmesan, Pecorino, salt, and pepper. Drain the pasta, reserving 1/2 cup of pasta water. Add the hot pasta to the pancetta and toss to combine. Remove from heat, then quickly mix in the egg and cheese mixture, adding a bit of pasta water if necessary to create a creamy sauce. Serve immediately, garnished with parsley.

Lasagna alla Bolognese

Ingredients:

- 12 lasagna noodles
- 1 lb ground beef
- 1/2 lb ground pork
- 1 onion, finely chopped
- 2 cloves garlic, minced
- 1 can (14 oz) crushed tomatoes
- 1/2 cup red wine
- 2 cups béchamel sauce (white sauce)
- 1 cup grated Parmesan cheese
- Salt and pepper to taste

Instructions:

Preheat the oven to 375°F (190°C). Cook the lasagna noodles according to package directions, then drain and set aside. In a large skillet, sauté the onion and garlic until soft. Add the ground beef and pork and cook until browned. Stir in the crushed tomatoes and red wine, and simmer for 30 minutes. In a baking dish, layer the noodles, Bolognese sauce, béchamel sauce, and Parmesan. Repeat the layers, ending with a layer of sauce and cheese. Bake for 45 minutes, then let it rest for 10 minutes before serving.

Risotto alla Milanese

Ingredients:

- 1 1/2 cups Arborio rice
- 4 cups chicken or vegetable broth
- 1/2 cup dry white wine
- 1 small onion, finely chopped
- 2 tablespoons butter
- 1/4 cup grated Parmesan cheese
- A pinch of saffron threads
- Salt and pepper to taste

Instructions:

In a small pot, warm the broth over low heat. In a large pan, melt the butter and sauté the onion until translucent. Add the rice and stir to coat with the butter. Pour in the white wine and cook, stirring, until the wine is absorbed. Add the saffron to the warm broth and stir it in. Gradually add the broth, one ladle at a time, stirring constantly and allowing the liquid to be absorbed before adding more. Continue until the rice is tender and creamy, about 18-20 minutes. Stir in the Parmesan, and season with salt and pepper before serving.

Caprese Salad

Ingredients:

- 3 ripe tomatoes, sliced
- 8 oz fresh mozzarella, sliced
- Fresh basil leaves
- Olive oil, for drizzling
- Balsamic vinegar (optional)
- Salt and pepper to taste

Instructions:

Arrange the tomato and mozzarella slices on a serving platter, alternating them with fresh basil leaves. Drizzle with olive oil and a touch of balsamic vinegar if desired. Season with salt and pepper, and serve immediately.

Fettuccine Alfredo

Ingredients:

- 12 oz fettuccine pasta
- 1/2 cup unsalted butter
- 1 cup heavy cream
- 1 1/2 cups grated Parmesan cheese
- Salt and pepper to taste
- Fresh parsley, for garnish

Instructions:

Cook the fettuccine according to package instructions. In a large pan, melt the butter over medium heat and stir in the heavy cream. Simmer for a few minutes until the sauce thickens slightly. Add the grated Parmesan and stir until melted and creamy. Season with salt and pepper. Toss the cooked fettuccine in the sauce and serve garnished with fresh parsley.

Gnocchi with Pesto

Ingredients:

- 1 lb potato gnocchi (store-bought or homemade)
- 1/2 cup pesto sauce
- 1 tablespoon olive oil
- Fresh Parmesan cheese, for garnish

Instructions:

Cook the gnocchi in a large pot of salted boiling water according to package instructions. Once they float to the surface, remove them with a slotted spoon and set aside. In a large pan, heat the pesto sauce and olive oil. Add the cooked gnocchi and toss to coat. Serve with freshly grated Parmesan.

Osso Buco

Ingredients:

- 4 veal shanks
- 1 onion, finely chopped
- 2 carrots, diced
- 2 celery stalks, diced
- 2 cloves garlic, minced
- 1 cup dry white wine
- 1 can (14 oz) crushed tomatoes
- 2 cups beef broth
- 1 teaspoon dried thyme
- 1 tablespoon chopped parsley (for gremolata)
- Zest of 1 lemon (for gremolata)

Instructions:

Preheat the oven to 350°F (175°C). In a large Dutch oven, brown the veal shanks on all sides. Remove and set aside. In the same pot, sauté the onion, carrots, celery, and garlic until softened. Pour in the white wine and let it reduce by half. Add the crushed tomatoes, beef broth, and thyme. Return the veal shanks to the pot and cover. Cook in the oven for 2-3 hours until the meat is tender. For the gremolata, mix the parsley and lemon zest. Serve the osso buco with a sprinkle of gremolata.

Eggplant Parmesan

Ingredients:

- 2 medium eggplants, sliced into 1/2-inch rounds
- 2 cups marinara sauce
- 2 cups mozzarella cheese, shredded
- 1/2 cup grated Parmesan cheese
- 1 cup breadcrumbs
- 1/4 cup flour
- 2 eggs, beaten
- Olive oil, for frying

Instructions:

Preheat the oven to 375°F (190°C). Dip each eggplant slice in flour, then egg, and finally breadcrumbs. Heat olive oil in a skillet and fry the eggplant slices until golden on both sides. In a baking dish, layer the fried eggplant with marinara sauce, mozzarella, and Parmesan cheese. Repeat the layers and top with cheese. Bake for 25-30 minutes, until the cheese is bubbly and golden.

Tiramisu

Ingredients:

- 6 egg yolks
- 3/4 cup sugar
- 1 1/4 cups mascarpone cheese
- 1 cup heavy cream
- 1 teaspoon vanilla extract
- 1 1/2 cups strong coffee, cooled
- 1/4 cup rum (optional)
- 24 ladyfinger cookies
- Cocoa powder, for dusting

Instructions:

In a bowl, whisk together the egg yolks and sugar until light and fluffy. Add the mascarpone and vanilla extract and mix until smooth. In a separate bowl, whip the heavy cream until stiff peaks form, then fold it into the mascarpone mixture. In a shallow dish, combine the coffee and rum. Dip the ladyfingers into the coffee mixture and layer them in a baking dish. Spread half of the mascarpone mixture on top and repeat the layers. Refrigerate for at least 4 hours. Dust with cocoa powder before serving.

Bruschetta with Tomatoes and Basil

Ingredients:

- 1 loaf of Italian baguette or crusty bread
- 4 ripe tomatoes, diced
- 1/4 cup fresh basil, chopped
- 2 cloves garlic, minced
- Olive oil, for drizzling
- Salt and pepper to taste

Instructions:

Preheat the oven to 400°F (200°C). Slice the bread into 1-inch thick pieces and place them on a baking sheet. Toast the bread in the oven for about 5-7 minutes, or until golden and crispy. In a bowl, combine the diced tomatoes, basil, garlic, salt, and pepper. Drizzle olive oil over the toasted bread slices, then top with the tomato mixture. Serve immediately.

Frittata with Spinach and Cheese

Ingredients:

- 8 large eggs
- 1 cup fresh spinach, chopped
- 1/2 cup grated Parmesan cheese
- 1/2 cup shredded mozzarella cheese
- 1 small onion, chopped
- 2 tablespoons olive oil
- Salt and pepper to taste

Instructions:

Preheat the oven to 375°F (190°C). Heat olive oil in an oven-safe skillet and sauté the onion until soft. Add the spinach and cook until wilted. In a bowl, whisk together the eggs, Parmesan, mozzarella, salt, and pepper. Pour the egg mixture into the skillet and cook for 3-4 minutes over medium heat. Transfer the skillet to the oven and bake for 8-10 minutes, or until the frittata is set and golden. Serve warm or at room temperature.

Vitello Tonnato

Ingredients:

- 1 lb veal roast
- 2 cups chicken broth
- 1/2 cup white wine
- 1/2 cup canned tuna, drained
- 1/4 cup mayonnaise
- 1 tablespoon capers
- 2 tablespoons lemon juice
- Salt and pepper to taste

Instructions:

Cook the veal roast by simmering it in a pot with chicken broth and white wine for about 1-1.5 hours, until the meat is tender. Allow the veal to cool completely. In a food processor, blend together the tuna, mayonnaise, capers, lemon juice, salt, and pepper to create the sauce. Slice the veal thinly and arrange the slices on a platter. Spoon the tuna sauce over the veal and chill before serving.

Panzanella Salad

Ingredients:

- 4 cups stale bread, cubed
- 3 ripe tomatoes, chopped
- 1 cucumber, diced
- 1/4 red onion, thinly sliced
- 1/4 cup fresh basil, chopped
- 1/4 cup red wine vinegar
- 1/4 cup olive oil
- Salt and pepper to taste

Instructions:

Soak the bread cubes in water for 5-10 minutes, then squeeze out excess moisture. In a large bowl, combine the bread, tomatoes, cucumber, onion, and basil. In a small bowl, whisk together the red wine vinegar, olive oil, salt, and pepper. Pour the dressing over the salad and toss gently. Let it sit for 30 minutes to allow the flavors to meld, then serve.

Ravioli with Ricotta and Spinach

Ingredients:

- 1 package fresh ravioli (or homemade ravioli)
- 2 cups ricotta cheese
- 1 cup cooked spinach, chopped
- 1 tablespoon olive oil
- 1 clove garlic, minced
- 1/2 cup grated Parmesan cheese
- Salt and pepper to taste

Instructions:

Cook the ravioli according to the package instructions. In a skillet, heat olive oil and sauté the garlic for 1-2 minutes until fragrant. Add the spinach and cook for another 2-3 minutes. In a bowl, mix the ricotta, Parmesan, salt, and pepper. Once the ravioli is cooked, toss it with the spinach and ricotta mixture in the skillet until well combined. Serve with extra Parmesan on top.

Minestrone Soup

Ingredients:

- 1 tablespoon olive oil
- 1 onion, chopped
- 2 carrots, diced
- 2 celery stalks, diced
- 2 cloves garlic, minced
- 1 zucchini, chopped
- 1 can (14 oz) diced tomatoes
- 4 cups vegetable broth
- 1 cup small pasta (like elbow or ditalini)
- 1 cup cooked beans (cannellini or kidney)
- Fresh basil, for garnish
- Salt and pepper to taste

Instructions:

Heat olive oil in a large pot and sauté the onion, carrots, celery, and garlic until softened, about 5 minutes. Add the zucchini and cook for an additional 3 minutes. Stir in the diced tomatoes, vegetable broth, and pasta. Bring to a simmer and cook until the pasta is tender, about 10-12 minutes. Add the beans and cook for 5 more minutes. Season with salt and pepper. Serve garnished with fresh basil.

Focaccia Bread

Ingredients:

- 2 1/4 cups all-purpose flour
- 1 tablespoon sugar
- 1 tablespoon active dry yeast
- 1 cup warm water
- 1/4 cup olive oil
- 1 teaspoon salt
- Fresh rosemary, for topping
- Coarse sea salt, for topping

Instructions:

In a bowl, combine the warm water, sugar, and yeast. Let it sit for 5 minutes until frothy. In a separate bowl, mix the flour, salt, olive oil, and yeast mixture. Knead the dough for 5-7 minutes until smooth. Place the dough in an oiled bowl, cover, and let it rise for 1 hour. Preheat the oven to 400°F (200°C). Once the dough has risen, press it out onto a baking sheet. Top with rosemary and sea salt. Bake for 20-25 minutes, or until golden and crispy.

Polenta with Mushrooms

Ingredients:

- 1 cup cornmeal (for polenta)
- 4 cups water or vegetable broth
- 2 tablespoons butter
- 1 cup mushrooms, sliced
- 2 tablespoons olive oil
- 2 cloves garlic, minced
- 1/4 cup grated Parmesan cheese
- Salt and pepper to taste

Instructions:

Bring the water or broth to a boil in a large pot. Slowly whisk in the cornmeal and cook, stirring frequently, until the polenta thickens and pulls away from the sides, about 20-25 minutes. Stir in the butter and Parmesan cheese, then season with salt and pepper. Meanwhile, heat olive oil in a skillet and sauté the mushrooms and garlic until tender, about 5 minutes. Serve the polenta topped with sautéed mushrooms.

Marinated Artichokes

Ingredients:

- 6 fresh artichokes
- 1 cup olive oil
- 1/4 cup red wine vinegar
- 2 cloves garlic, minced
- 1 tablespoon fresh parsley, chopped
- 1 teaspoon lemon zest
- 1/2 teaspoon dried oregano
- Salt and pepper to taste

Instructions:

Trim the artichokes, removing the tough outer leaves and cutting off the tops. Steam the artichokes for about 20-30 minutes until tender. Allow them to cool. In a bowl, mix the olive oil, red wine vinegar, garlic, parsley, lemon zest, oregano, salt, and pepper. Slice the artichokes and place them in a jar or container. Pour the marinade over the artichokes and refrigerate for at least 4 hours before serving.

Cacciatore Chicken

Ingredients:

- 4 chicken thighs or breasts
- 1 tablespoon olive oil
- 1 onion, chopped
- 2 cloves garlic, minced
- 1 cup crushed tomatoes
- 1/2 cup dry white wine
- 1/2 cup chicken broth
- 1/4 cup olives, pitted and chopped
- 1 teaspoon dried oregano
- 1 teaspoon dried rosemary
- Salt and pepper to taste

Instructions:

Heat olive oil in a large skillet over medium heat. Season the chicken with salt and pepper, then brown on both sides for 5-7 minutes. Remove the chicken and set aside. In the same skillet, sauté the onion and garlic until softened. Add the crushed tomatoes, white wine, chicken broth, olives, oregano, and rosemary. Bring to a simmer. Return the chicken to the skillet, cover, and cook for 25-30 minutes until the chicken is cooked through. Serve with a side of vegetables or pasta.

Bucatini all'Amatriciana

Ingredients:

- 12 oz bucatini pasta
- 4 oz guanciale (or pancetta), diced
- 1 can (14 oz) crushed tomatoes
- 1/2 teaspoon red pepper flakes
- 1/4 cup Pecorino Romano cheese, grated
- 1 tablespoon olive oil
- Salt to taste

Instructions:

Cook the bucatini pasta according to the package instructions. While the pasta cooks, heat olive oil in a large skillet over medium heat. Add the guanciale and cook until crispy, about 5 minutes. Add the red pepper flakes and crushed tomatoes, then simmer for 10-15 minutes. Once the pasta is done, drain and toss it with the sauce. Sprinkle with Pecorino Romano and serve.

Arancini (Stuffed Rice Balls)

Ingredients:

- 2 cups cooked risotto (preferably chilled)
- 1/2 cup mozzarella cheese, cubed
- 1/4 cup grated Parmesan cheese
- 1 egg, beaten
- 1/4 cup flour
- 1 cup breadcrumbs
- Vegetable oil for frying
- Salt to taste

Instructions:

Form the cold risotto into small balls, placing a cube of mozzarella in the center of each. Dip each rice ball into the beaten egg, then roll in flour and breadcrumbs to coat. Heat oil in a frying pan over medium heat. Fry the arancini in batches until golden brown and crispy, about 4-5 minutes. Drain on paper towels and serve with marinara sauce for dipping.

Cannoli

Ingredients:

- 12 cannoli shells (store-bought or homemade)
- 2 cups ricotta cheese
- 1 cup powdered sugar
- 1/2 teaspoon vanilla extract
- 1/2 cup mini chocolate chips
- 1/4 cup candied orange peel (optional)

Instructions:

In a bowl, combine the ricotta cheese, powdered sugar, and vanilla extract. Mix until smooth. Fill a pastry bag with the ricotta mixture and pipe it into the cannoli shells. Garnish with mini chocolate chips and candied orange peel. Serve chilled.

Ricotta Cheesecake

Ingredients:

- 2 cups ricotta cheese
- 1 cup cream cheese, softened
- 1/2 cup sugar
- 1 teaspoon vanilla extract
- 3 large eggs
- 1/4 cup all-purpose flour
- 1/2 cup heavy cream

Instructions:

Preheat the oven to 325°F (160°C). In a mixing bowl, combine the ricotta, cream cheese, sugar, and vanilla extract. Add the eggs, one at a time, mixing well after each. Stir in the flour and heavy cream. Pour the mixture into a greased cheesecake pan and bake for 50-60 minutes, until set. Let it cool before refrigerating for several hours. Serve chilled.

Porchetta

Ingredients:

- 3-4 lbs pork belly or pork loin with skin on
- 4 cloves garlic, minced
- 2 tablespoons fresh rosemary, chopped
- 1 tablespoon fennel seeds
- 1 tablespoon olive oil
- Salt and pepper to taste

Instructions:

Preheat the oven to 400°F (200°C). Score the skin of the pork and rub with olive oil, garlic, rosemary, fennel seeds, salt, and pepper. Roll up the pork, securing it with kitchen twine. Place the porchetta on a roasting rack and roast for 20 minutes. Lower the temperature to 325°F (165°C) and continue roasting for 2-3 hours, until the pork is tender and the skin is crispy. Let rest before slicing and serving.

Farro Salad with Vegetables

Ingredients:

- 1 cup farro, cooked
- 1 cup cherry tomatoes, halved
- 1 cucumber, diced
- 1/4 red onion, thinly sliced
- 1/4 cup fresh parsley, chopped
- 1/4 cup olive oil
- 2 tablespoons red wine vinegar
- Salt and pepper to taste

Instructions:

In a large bowl, combine the cooked farro, tomatoes, cucumber, onion, and parsley. In a small bowl, whisk together the olive oil, red wine vinegar, salt, and pepper. Pour the dressing over the salad and toss to combine. Serve chilled or at room temperature.

Sicilian Caponata

Ingredients:

- 1 eggplant, diced
- 1 onion, chopped
- 2 stalks celery, chopped
- 1/4 cup green olives, pitted and chopped
- 1/4 cup capers
- 1 can (14 oz) diced tomatoes
- 1/4 cup red wine vinegar
- 2 tablespoons sugar
- Olive oil for frying
- Salt and pepper to taste

Instructions:

In a large skillet, heat olive oil over medium heat. Fry the eggplant until golden and tender, then remove and set aside. In the same skillet, sauté the onion and celery until soft. Add the olives, capers, tomatoes, vinegar, and sugar, and cook for 10-15 minutes. Stir in the fried eggplant and season with salt and pepper. Serve at room temperature or chilled.

Pasta Primavera

Ingredients:

- 12 oz pasta (spaghetti or penne)
- 2 tablespoons olive oil
- 1 small onion, chopped
- 2 cloves garlic, minced
- 1 red bell pepper, thinly sliced
- 1 zucchini, sliced
- 1 cup cherry tomatoes, halved
- 1/2 cup fresh basil, chopped
- 1/2 cup Parmesan cheese, grated
- Salt and pepper to taste

Instructions:

Cook the pasta according to package directions. While the pasta cooks, heat olive oil in a large pan over medium heat. Sauté the onion and garlic until fragrant. Add the bell pepper, zucchini, and tomatoes, and cook for about 5 minutes until tender. Drain the pasta and toss it with the sautéed vegetables. Add fresh basil, grated Parmesan, and season with salt and pepper. Serve hot.

Risotto with Seafood

Ingredients:

- 1 cup Arborio rice
- 1/2 onion, chopped
- 2 tablespoons olive oil
- 2 cloves garlic, minced
- 1/2 cup white wine
- 4 cups seafood stock
- 1 cup mixed seafood (shrimp, mussels, squid)
- 1/4 cup fresh parsley, chopped
- 1 tablespoon butter
- Salt and pepper to taste

Instructions:

In a large pan, heat olive oil over medium heat and sauté the onion and garlic until soft. Add the rice and cook for 1-2 minutes. Pour in the white wine and cook until absorbed. Gradually add the seafood stock, one ladle at a time, stirring constantly until the rice is creamy and al dente. In a separate pan, cook the seafood until just done. Stir the seafood, parsley, butter, salt, and pepper into the risotto. Serve immediately.

Pappardelle with Wild Boar Ragù

Ingredients:

- 12 oz pappardelle pasta
- 2 tablespoons olive oil
- 1 lb wild boar, diced
- 1 onion, chopped
- 2 cloves garlic, minced
- 1 cup red wine
- 1 can (14 oz) crushed tomatoes
- 1 teaspoon dried rosemary
- Salt and pepper to taste
- Fresh parsley for garnish

Instructions:

Cook the pappardelle pasta according to package directions. Heat olive oil in a large pan over medium heat and brown the wild boar. Remove the boar and set it aside. In the same pan, sauté the onion and garlic until soft. Add the wine, scraping up any bits from the pan. Stir in the tomatoes, rosemary, salt, and pepper. Return the wild boar to the pan, cover, and simmer for 1-1.5 hours until the meat is tender. Toss the ragù with the pasta and garnish with fresh parsley. Serve hot.

Zuppa Toscana

Ingredients:

- 1 lb Italian sausage, crumbled
- 4 large potatoes, sliced
- 1 onion, chopped
- 3 cloves garlic, minced
- 6 cups chicken broth
- 1 bunch kale, chopped
- 1/2 cup heavy cream
- Salt and pepper to taste
- Red pepper flakes (optional)

Instructions:

In a large pot, cook the sausage until browned. Remove and set aside. In the same pot, sauté the onion and garlic until fragrant. Add the potatoes and chicken broth, and bring to a boil. Reduce heat and simmer until the potatoes are tender, about 10-15 minutes. Stir in the cooked sausage, kale, heavy cream, salt, pepper, and red pepper flakes. Simmer for an additional 5 minutes. Serve warm.

Semifreddo

Ingredients:

- 1 cup heavy cream
- 1/2 cup sugar
- 4 egg yolks
- 1 teaspoon vanilla extract
- 1/4 cup chopped pistachios (optional)

Instructions:

In a bowl, whisk together the egg yolks and sugar until thick. In a separate bowl, whip the cream until soft peaks form. Gently fold the whipped cream into the egg mixture. Add the vanilla extract and pistachios, if using. Pour the mixture into a loaf pan and freeze for at least 4 hours. Slice and serve.

Neapolitan Pizza Margherita

Ingredients:

- 1 pizza dough (store-bought or homemade)
- 1/2 cup tomato sauce
- 8 oz fresh mozzarella, sliced
- Fresh basil leaves
- Olive oil for drizzling
- Salt to taste

Instructions:

Preheat the oven to 475°F (245°C). Roll out the pizza dough on a floured surface. Spread the tomato sauce evenly on the dough. Place the mozzarella slices on top and sprinkle with salt. Bake for 10-12 minutes until the crust is golden and the cheese is bubbly. Remove from the oven and top with fresh basil leaves and a drizzle of olive oil. Serve hot.

Baked Ziti

Ingredients:

- 12 oz ziti pasta
- 2 cups marinara sauce
- 1 lb ricotta cheese
- 1 cup mozzarella cheese, shredded
- 1/4 cup Parmesan cheese, grated
- 1/4 cup fresh basil, chopped

Instructions:

Preheat the oven to 375°F (190°C). Cook the ziti according to package instructions. In a large bowl, combine the cooked pasta, marinara sauce, ricotta, mozzarella, and Parmesan. Pour the mixture into a baking dish and top with the remaining mozzarella. Bake for 25-30 minutes until golden and bubbly. Garnish with fresh basil and serve.

Cicchetti (Venetian Tapas)

Ingredients:

- 1/2 cup cooked shrimp, chopped
- 1/2 cup fresh mozzarella, diced
- 1/4 cup olive tapenade
- 1 baguette, sliced
- Fresh herbs (parsley, basil) for garnish

Instructions:

Arrange the baguette slices on a baking sheet and toast them in the oven until golden. Top each slice with a dollop of olive tapenade, a piece of mozzarella, and some chopped shrimp. Garnish with fresh herbs and serve as small tapas-style appetizers.

Stuffed Zucchini Flowers

Ingredients:

- 12 zucchini flowers, cleaned and trimmed
- 1/2 cup ricotta cheese
- 1/4 cup Parmesan cheese, grated
- 1 tablespoon fresh basil, chopped
- 1 egg, beaten
- 1/2 cup flour
- Vegetable oil for frying
- Salt and pepper to taste

Instructions:

Mix the ricotta, Parmesan, basil, salt, and pepper in a bowl. Carefully stuff each zucchini flower with the mixture. Dip each stuffed flower in flour, then into the beaten egg. Heat vegetable oil in a frying pan over medium heat and fry the flowers until golden and crispy, about 2-3 minutes per side. Drain on paper towels and serve hot.

Gnocchi alla Sorrentina

Ingredients:

- 1 lb potato gnocchi
- 2 cups marinara sauce
- 1/2 cup mozzarella cheese, shredded
- 1/4 cup Parmesan cheese, grated
- Fresh basil leaves for garnish

Instructions:

Preheat the oven to 375°F (190°C). Cook the gnocchi according to package directions, then drain. In a baking dish, layer the cooked gnocchi, marinara sauce, and mozzarella cheese. Sprinkle with Parmesan cheese. Bake for 15-20 minutes until bubbly and golden. Garnish with fresh basil and serve hot.

Sicilian Cannoli

Ingredients:

- 12 cannoli shells (store-bought or homemade)
- 1 1/2 cups ricotta cheese
- 1/2 cup powdered sugar
- 1 teaspoon vanilla extract
- 1/2 cup mini chocolate chips
- 1/4 cup chopped pistachios (optional)
- Powdered sugar for dusting

Instructions:

In a mixing bowl, combine the ricotta cheese, powdered sugar, and vanilla extract. Mix until smooth. Fold in mini chocolate chips and chopped pistachios (if using). Fill the cannoli shells with the ricotta mixture using a piping bag. Dust with powdered sugar before serving. Serve chilled.

Torta della Nonna

Ingredients:

- 1 package puff pastry (store-bought or homemade)
- 1 1/2 cups pastry cream (custard)
- 1/4 cup pine nuts
- Powdered sugar for dusting
- 1 egg, beaten (for brushing)

Instructions:

Preheat the oven to 375°F (190°C). Roll out the puff pastry and line a tart pan with it. Pour the pastry cream into the pastry shell and smooth it out. Sprinkle pine nuts on top. Brush the edges of the pastry with beaten egg. Bake for 25-30 minutes until the pastry is golden and the pine nuts are toasted. Let cool, then dust with powdered sugar before serving.

Carbonara with Pecorino Romano

Ingredients:

- 12 oz spaghetti
- 4 oz guanciale (or pancetta), diced
- 3 large eggs
- 1/2 cup Pecorino Romano cheese, grated
- Salt and freshly ground black pepper to taste

Instructions:

Cook the spaghetti according to package directions. In a large skillet, cook the guanciale over medium heat until crispy, about 5-7 minutes. In a bowl, whisk together the eggs, Pecorino Romano, salt, and pepper. When the pasta is cooked, reserve 1/2 cup of pasta water and then drain the pasta. Add the hot pasta to the guanciale and toss to combine. Remove from heat and slowly stir in the egg mixture, adding reserved pasta water to create a creamy sauce. Serve immediately.

Fagioli all'Uccelletto

Ingredients:

- 2 cups cannellini beans, cooked or canned
- 1 tablespoon olive oil
- 2 cloves garlic, minced
- 1/2 teaspoon dried sage
- 1/2 teaspoon red pepper flakes
- 1 can (14 oz) crushed tomatoes
- Salt and pepper to taste

Instructions:

In a large pan, heat olive oil over medium heat. Sauté the garlic, sage, and red pepper flakes until fragrant. Add the crushed tomatoes and simmer for 10 minutes. Stir in the cooked cannellini beans and simmer for another 5-10 minutes. Season with salt and pepper to taste. Serve warm.

Italian Meatballs in Marinara Sauce

Ingredients:

- 1 lb ground beef
- 1/4 cup breadcrumbs
- 1/4 cup grated Parmesan cheese
- 1 egg
- 2 cloves garlic, minced
- 1/4 cup fresh parsley, chopped
- Salt and pepper to taste
- 2 cups marinara sauce

Instructions:

In a large bowl, mix together the ground beef, breadcrumbs, Parmesan, egg, garlic, parsley, salt, and pepper. Form the mixture into meatballs. Heat olive oil in a skillet and brown the meatballs on all sides. Once browned, add the marinara sauce to the pan and simmer for 15-20 minutes, until the meatballs are cooked through. Serve with pasta or crusty bread.

Pasta alla Norma

Ingredients:

- 12 oz pasta (rigatoni or spaghetti)
- 2 medium eggplants, diced
- 3 tablespoons olive oil
- 2 cloves garlic, minced
- 1 can (14 oz) crushed tomatoes
- 1/2 teaspoon dried oregano
- 1/4 cup fresh basil, chopped
- Salt and pepper to taste
- 1/2 cup ricotta salata cheese, grated

Instructions:

Cook the pasta according to package directions. While the pasta is cooking, heat olive oil in a pan over medium heat and sauté the eggplant until golden and tender, about 10 minutes. Add the garlic and cook for 1 minute, then stir in the crushed tomatoes, oregano, salt, and pepper. Simmer for 10 minutes. Drain the pasta and toss with the sauce. Top with ricotta salata and fresh basil. Serve hot.

Baked Eggplant with Tomato Sauce

Ingredients:

- 2 medium eggplants, sliced into rounds
- 2 cups marinara sauce
- 1/2 cup mozzarella cheese, shredded
- 1/4 cup Parmesan cheese, grated
- 1/4 cup fresh basil, chopped
- Olive oil for drizzling
- Salt and pepper to taste

Instructions:

Preheat the oven to 375°F (190°C). Arrange the eggplant slices on a baking sheet and drizzle with olive oil. Season with salt and pepper. Bake for 25-30 minutes until tender. Top each eggplant slice with marinara sauce, mozzarella, and Parmesan. Return to the oven and bake for an additional 10 minutes until the cheese is melted and bubbly. Garnish with fresh basil before serving.

Saffron Risotto with Shrimp

Ingredients:

- 1 lb shrimp, peeled and deveined
- 1 1/2 cups Arborio rice
- 1/2 teaspoon saffron threads
- 4 cups chicken broth
- 1/2 cup dry white wine
- 1 medium onion, finely chopped
- 2 cloves garlic, minced
- 2 tablespoons olive oil
- 1/4 cup Parmesan cheese, grated
- Salt and freshly ground black pepper to taste
- 2 tablespoons fresh parsley, chopped

Instructions:

In a small bowl, steep the saffron threads in a little warm water and set aside. In a saucepan, heat the chicken broth over low heat. In a large skillet, heat olive oil over medium heat. Add the onion and garlic, sautéing until softened. Add the rice and cook for 2 minutes, stirring occasionally. Pour in the white wine and cook until the wine is absorbed. Begin adding the warm chicken broth, one ladleful at a time, stirring frequently and allowing the liquid to be absorbed before adding more. After about 15 minutes, stir in the saffron infusion and continue cooking until the rice is tender and creamy (about 20 minutes). In a separate pan, cook the shrimp until pink, about 2-3 minutes per side. Stir the shrimp into the risotto, then remove from heat and mix in the Parmesan cheese. Season with salt, pepper, and fresh parsley before serving.

Pizzelle (Italian Waffle Cookies)

Ingredients:

- 2 cups all-purpose flour
- 1 teaspoon baking powder
- 1/2 teaspoon vanilla extract
- 1/2 teaspoon anise extract (optional)
- 4 large eggs
- 1 cup sugar
- 1/2 cup unsalted butter, melted
- 1/4 cup vegetable oil

Instructions:

Preheat your pizzelle maker according to the manufacturer's instructions. In a bowl, whisk together the flour and baking powder. In another bowl, beat the eggs and sugar together until light and fluffy. Add the melted butter, vegetable oil, vanilla, and anise extract, mixing until combined. Gradually add the flour mixture, stirring until the batter is smooth. Spoon the batter onto the preheated pizzelle maker, close the lid, and cook for about 1-2 minutes until golden. Remove the cookies and let cool. Dust with powdered sugar if desired before serving.

Saltimbocca alla Romana

Ingredients:

- 4 veal cutlets (or chicken breasts)
- 4 slices prosciutto
- 8 fresh sage leaves
- 2 tablespoons olive oil
- 1/2 cup dry white wine
- 1/2 cup chicken broth
- Salt and freshly ground black pepper to taste
- 2 tablespoons butter

Instructions:

Place a slice of prosciutto and 2 sage leaves on each veal cutlet. Use toothpicks to secure the prosciutto and sage in place. Heat olive oil in a skillet over medium-high heat. Add the veal cutlets and cook for 3-4 minutes per side until golden and cooked through. Remove the veal from the skillet and set aside. In the same skillet, add the white wine and chicken broth, scraping up any browned bits from the pan. Let the sauce reduce for 2-3 minutes. Stir in the butter until melted and the sauce is smooth. Return the veal to the pan, spooning the sauce over the top. Serve hot.

Limoncello Sorbet

Ingredients:

- 1 1/2 cups water
- 1 cup sugar
- 1 cup fresh lemon juice
- 1 tablespoon lemon zest
- 1/2 cup Limoncello liqueur

Instructions:

In a saucepan, combine the water and sugar. Bring to a simmer, stirring until the sugar dissolves. Remove from heat and allow to cool. Stir in the fresh lemon juice, lemon zest, and Limoncello. Pour the mixture into a shallow dish and place in the freezer. Every 30 minutes, use a fork to scrape and stir the mixture to break up any ice crystals. Continue this process for 3-4 hours, or until the sorbet is frozen and fluffy. Serve in chilled bowls.

Insalata di Mare (Seafood Salad)

Ingredients:

- 1/2 lb shrimp, peeled and deveined
- 1/2 lb squid, cleaned and sliced into rings
- 1/2 lb scallops, cleaned
- 1/2 cup cherry tomatoes, halved
- 1/4 red onion, thinly sliced
- 2 tablespoons fresh parsley, chopped
- 2 tablespoons lemon juice
- 2 tablespoons olive oil
- Salt and freshly ground black pepper to taste

Instructions:

In a large pot of salted boiling water, cook the shrimp, squid, and scallops until just cooked through, about 2-3 minutes. Drain and transfer the seafood to a bowl of ice water to cool. Once cooled, drain again and place the seafood in a mixing bowl. Add the cherry tomatoes, red onion, and parsley. Drizzle with lemon juice and olive oil, and toss to combine. Season with salt and pepper to taste. Serve chilled.

Cantucci with Vin Santo

Ingredients:

- 2 cups all-purpose flour
- 1 cup sugar
- 1/2 teaspoon baking powder
- 2 large eggs
- 1 teaspoon vanilla extract
- 1/2 teaspoon almond extract
- 1 cup whole almonds, toasted

Instructions:

Preheat the oven to 350°F (175°C). In a mixing bowl, combine the flour, sugar, and baking powder. In another bowl, whisk together the eggs, vanilla, and almond extract. Gradually add the dry ingredients to the wet ingredients, stirring until a dough forms. Fold in the toasted almonds. Divide the dough into two logs and place them on a baking sheet lined with parchment paper. Bake for 25-30 minutes until golden. Remove from the oven and let cool for 10 minutes. Slice the logs into 1/2-inch thick cookies and return to the oven to bake for an additional 10-12 minutes until crisp. Serve with Vin Santo for dipping.

www.ingramcontent.com/pod-product-compliance
Lightning Source LLC
LaVergne TN
LVHW081508060526
838201LV00056BA/3003